The Bat Book

by Hugh Warwick

Photography by Daniel Hargreaves
Series editor Jane Russ

Dedications

Without the millions of midges and mosquitoes, there would be no bats. So this book is dedicated to all those little beasties we have sworn at on a summer's evening!

Hugh Warwick

Contents

Introduction

Bats have not had the same success with public relations as hedgehogs, beavers or water voles but they are every bit as fascinating and even more extraordinary.

Bats are the only flying mammals. The fastest flying animal in the world is... a bat! Bats navigate and hunt using sound. A quarter of all species of mammal in the UK are bats. They hibernate, they indicate the health of our environment and they eat insects, lots and lots of them. They carry more folklore, mythology and downright nonsense than any other animal.
Bats are amazing.

Left: Roosting lesser horseshoe bat.

Daubenton's bat.

What is a Bat?

What is a Bat?

This is a question that has taxed the great thinkers of history.

Ground-breaking naturalist the Comte de Buffon wrote in the late 18th century that the bat is 'half a quadruped and half a bird...a monstrous being... [an] imperfect quadruped and a still more imperfect bird.' This chimeric view of taxonomy was also used in a Germanic folk tale where the bat is taken to be Satan's failed attempt to make a replica of God's perfect swallow but messed up by including ears like a cat, a tail like a rat and leather wings.

Famously, the German for bat is actually *die fledermaus*, literally translated as flying or flitter mouse, though it is worth noting that bats are more closely related to humans than they are to mice.

Bats are mammals, like us. They have fur and are homeothermic. They give birth to live young and suckle them with milk but there the similarities end.

The most obvious difference is that they have wings and can fly. There are other mammals that manage to fall elegantly – for example, the flying squirrels, which have evolved a patagium, a furry flap of skin that acts as a parachute, enabling distances of up to 90m to be covered. However, this is not flying.

The Latin name given by taxonomists to bats gives a hint on how they do this. They are in the Kingdom Animalia and among them they are in the phylum Chordata, meaning they have a backbone.

Greater horseshoe bat
mother and pup.

Greater horseshoe bat hanging.

Greater horseshoe bat.

The Class is Mammalia and the next step into the detail of life is their Order, Chiroptera, and this is the big reveal, as that comes from Ancient Greek – χείρ – *cheir*, 'hand' and πτερόν – *pteron*, 'wing'.

So rather than a flap of skin extending from an arm, as in the squirrels, the hands of the bats have dramatically changed, their fine fingers linked together by thin skin. More on the mechanics and capabilities of these amazing hands later.

Something else that marks out the bat as different is how long they can live. For example, the common shrew, weighing around 9g, an animal that feeds on the same sort of food as bats, can be expected to live for 18 months. Some bats of similar size have been recorded as living 30-40 years. This is thought to be down in part to lower predation risk and also their ability to reduce the build up of toxins within cells that are responsible for much of the ageing process.

Bats are also extremely diverse, though we may not think that in the UK as our views tend to only ever be fleeting.

There are 17 species of bat that breed in Britain, making it our most common mammal, but that is just a small fraction of global bat diversity. There are over 1,400 species around the world, ranging in size from that of a bee, all the way up to a small dog! The largest flying foxes can have a wingspan of up to two metres and weigh 1.5kg. The appropriately named bumblebee bat weighs in at just two grams, considerably less than a five-pence piece.

In his book *The Blind Watchmaker*, Richard Dawkins says that to speak of bats as though they were all the same is like speaking of 'dogs, lions, weasels, bears, hyenas, pandas and otters all in one breath, just because they are all carnivores.'

Taxonomists, for a long time, split the bats into, basically, big and small, Megachiroptera and Microchiroptera. The big bats are the fruit bats of the tropics, while in Britain we only have the micros, the insect eaters.

Of course, taxonomists like to keep busy, so now the differentiation of bats is slightly different thanks to the evidence that comes from peaking into the genetics of these brilliant beasts. These studies revealed that the relationship between, for example, the horseshoe bats and fruit bats was closer than with other insect-eating micro bats. To be honest, the names were a little misleading as some of the largest micros are bigger than the smallest macros!

The Bat Conservation Trust explains, 'There are two alternative proposals for the new groupings of families of bats: Yinpterochiroptera and Yangochiroptera and Vespertilioniformes and

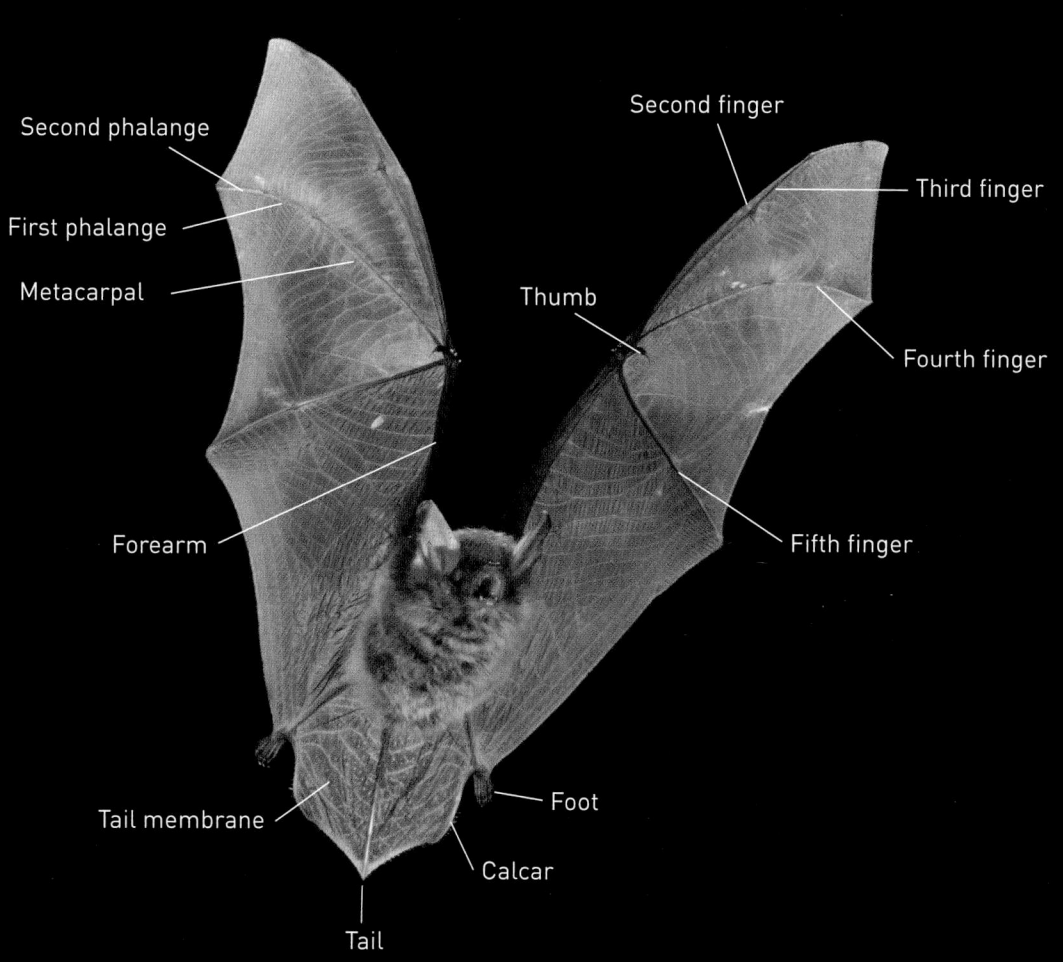

Second phalange

First phalange

Metacarpal

Forearm

Second finger

Third finger

Thumb

Fourth finger

Fifth finger

Tail membrane

Foot

Calcar

Tail

Soprano pipistrelle.

Pteropodiformes; currently researchers do not all agree which is correct and both sets of names are used.'

Overall, it is now believed that all bats have evolved from common ancestors that are more like our insect eaters – which means the mostly larger fruit-eating bats are the newcomers. The first ancestors of bats, so far identified, date back around 50 million years. However, it is very unlikely that these fossils represent the very first bats. In fact, molecular analysis leads experts to assume bats originally emerged shortly after the mass extinction event some 66 million years ago that saw the end of the dinosaurs, or even while there were still dinosaurs around. The space left by their demise allowed mammals of all shapes and sizes to start their ascendency.

Bats spend a lot of their lives upside down, hanging by their feet when they sleep or hibernate. This has

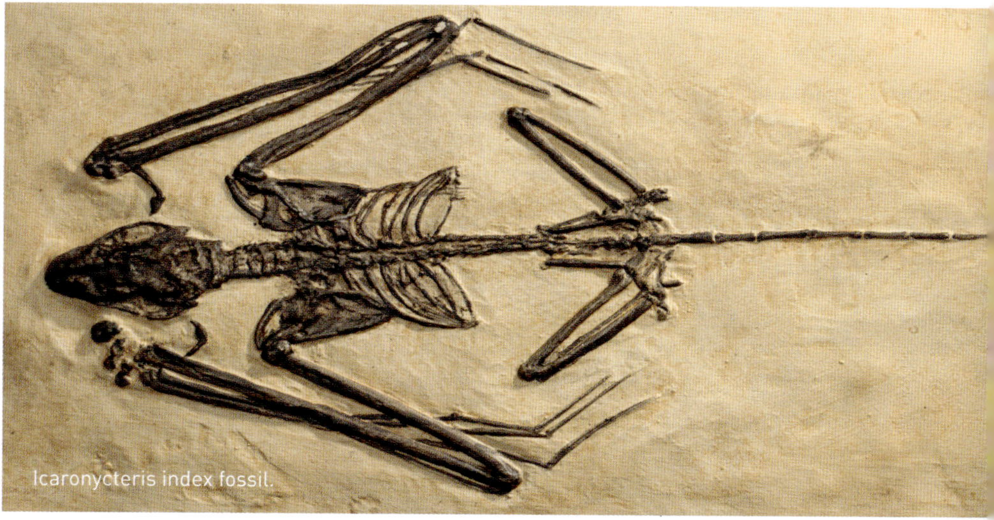

Icaronycteris index fossil.

resulted in remarkable adaptations – their feet face backwards and their knee joints are rotated upwards and outwards. Hanging is not energy expensive, not like a human holding on to a branch. For bats, the claws on their feet simply lock in place when the weight of the bat pulls down. This means that even dead bats dangle. This position means that take off for flight just requires letting go.

Hassianycteris messelensis fossil bat.

Greater mouse-eared bat.

Greater horseshoe pup.

British Bats

British Bats

The number of species of resident bats seems to have changed a lot over time but this is mostly due to bat experts realising that they had been inadvertently grouping different species together.

Most famously was the realisation that the **pipistrelle**, the commonest bat, was actually two species, the common and the soprano pipistrelle. It is not a great surprise to find that the soprano has a higher frequency echolocation call. But that is not it for pipistrelles. In 1997 it was found that the previously migrant species Nathusius' pipistrelle, which used to pop over the English Channel every now and then, had taken up residency.

There will be a deeper dive into echolocation soon, but just to explain, one of the easiest ways to differentiate species of bat is by the frequency of the sounds they make for hunting and navigation – hence its use to discover different species.

While there are 17 species of bat that are resident breeders in the UK, there is an 18th, the greater mouse-eared bat. Although declared extinct in the UK in 1992, single individuals are occasionally found hibernating in the southeast and there are hopes for recovery.

We can split our bats into two groups. There are two **horseshoe bats**, the greater (*Rhinolophus ferrumequinum*) and lesser

The three pipistrelle species.

Greater horseshoe face.

Lesser horseshoe bat.

The noseleaf of a greater horseshoe bat.

Lesser horseshoe bat hibernating.

Ear notch

Ear

Tragus

Muzzle

Nostrils

Vesper face diagram.

(*R. hipposideros*). These bats are distinguished by their complex 'noseleaves', folds of skin on their face that help direct the sound they emit for echolocation.

It will be no surprise that the difference between them is size – the greater weighing up to 34g, making it one of our bigger bats and the lesser just making it to 9g and, in turn, being one of our smallest bats.

Then there are the 15 species of **Vesper bats** – for those with a memory of church services, this name should become clear, as vespers were the evening prayer (the word is Latin for evening). These bats are known as 'simple nosed' – which they most certainly are when compared to the wonderful faces of the horseshoe bats.

These evening bats in the UK are made up of three broad groupings.

The genus **Myotis**, which consists of six breeding species: whiskered, Brandt's, Alcathoe, Natterer's, Bechstein's, and Daubenton's.

Then there are the **Noctules, Pipistrelles** and allies consisting of another six species: the serotine, Leisler's, noctule and the three pips already mentioned.

Finally, there are the **long-eared bats**, which include the barbastelle, along with the brown and grey long-eared bats.

The horseshoe bats used to be cave dwellers, until we came along and started building them 'caves' galore in the form of rural houses and stables. Now they are rarely found in caves, at least during the summer.

Below: Myotis species in hand.

Grey long-eared bat.

Noctule.

Brown long-eared bat.

As the temperature drops and they seek somewhere to hibernate they do revert back and head underground, either in caves or mines. Both horseshoe bats are rare in the UK.

Myotis means 'mouse eared', and in their ears, if you are really close by, you will see the tragus, which for the Myotis bats is pointy.

The tragus is the bit of cartilage that grows in front of the ear, found in humans and bats. For humans the tragus assists in collecting sound from behind. In bats, or at least in those with a tragus, this prominence allows for increased subtlety in echolocation, the tragus providing enhanced capacity to vertically discriminate objects around them. Studies where the tragus has been temporarily glued into a different position have resulted in a 25% reduction in navigational acuity.

The most common bat in the UK is the common pipistrelle. The pips, as they are known, are also the smallest of our bats, weighing just 5g, the same as a 20p piece.

The long-eared bats have, and it will not come as a surprise, long ears, the cutest of them all being the brown long-eared bat, who also has freckles.

Left: Common pipistrelle.
Right: Brown long-eared bat.

Alcathoe bat

Barbastelle

Bechstein's bat

Brandt's bat

Brown long-eared bat

Common pipistrelle

Daubenton's bat

Greater horseshoe bat

Grey long-eared bat

Leisler's bat

Lesser horseshoe bat

Nathusius's pipistrelle

Natterer's bat

Noctule bat

Serotine bat

Soprano pipistrelle

Whiskered bat

Greater mouse-eared bat

Brown long-eared bat and orange underwing moth.

What do Bats Eat and, More Importantly, How?

What do Bats Eat and, More Importantly, How?

As you already know, all the British bats are the micros – we have no flying foxes and fruit bats in the wild. We also have no vampire bats either. All UK bats eat insects.

We have around 20,000 species of insect so that suggests plenty of choice available to the bats. However, it is not quite that simple. Day-flying wasps and butterflies are mostly off the menu and the terrestrial bugs get away from their attentions too (though sometimes a beetle will be plucked from the ground). In addition, there are the noxious insects that have their own pharmacy of defence capabilities.

Not all bats get to feast on all the available insects either. Smaller species like the pipistrelles will not be able to catch the larger flying beetles, whereas the noctules have big and strong teeth and jaws designed to munch these with abandon.

Despite the limitations, the 17 different species breeding in the UK have a great variety in the details of the diet. Generally, it is macro invertebrates that are consumed, and they eat a lot. Flying uses a lot of energy, so they need to eat a lot of food, which they catch by flying.

A common pipistrelle can eat up to 3,000 insects in a night. If they are only hunting in the dark of a summer evening there might be six hours of activity, which means 500 insects an hour, which means over eight per minute. They do take rests throughout the night, so the intensity of the feeding effort could be even greater.

Grey long-eared bat eating
yellow underwing.

Bats mostly eat on the wing, although sometimes they will dangle upside down to eat larger items. When they do this we can get an insight into what they are actually eating. As you can imagine, with little pips skittering around trapping a midge every few seconds, recording what species they are is pretty much impossible, though there are ways – more on that in a moment.

The larger meals will often result in bits being discarded, such as wings and legs, and these can grow into an obvious pile. Given some patience and skill and a good guidebook, it is possible to use these to piece together who has been eaten.

Daubenton's bat over water.

Discarded moth wing collection.

Cockchafer (May bug).

Dung beetle.

For the smaller meals, plucked from the air by bats on the wing and eaten as they fly, working out the diet relies on the analysis of poo.

Droppings of bats are easiest to find beneath their roosts and sometimes these droppings are what bring these beautiful mammals into disrepute. Mainly this is due to the desire to keep some of the few old and accessible buildings free from the

reminders of who else lives there. Churches are a favoured haunt, as the high ceilings, often fashioned after forest glades, provide roosting opportunities. The church yards are usually allowed to remain green and will then attract bat food. Church wardens and the rota of volunteers who polish and clean do, in some instances, also curse their flighty neighbours.

The droppings on their own are not going to provide answers. You need to carefully spread them onto a glass slide and pop it under a microscope. Indigestible parts will be visible: legs, wings, scales, compound eyes and body cases. Phil Richardson describes it wonderfully, in his 1985 book called *Bats*, as a sort of self assembly kit, 'build your own beetle. Only 986 parts. No plans or glue provided.'

Though times are changing and now there is an easier way, through analysis of the DNA that can be recovered in the droppings. One recent study of Leisler's bats in Germany found an astonishing 358 species being eaten.

Single wild noctule dropping.

A world without bats would be a world which had already slipped over the edge into ecological collapse, bringing with it not just an absence of bats but also an absence of most life on Earth.

These were made up of 126 species of moth, 86 flies and mosquitoes, 48 species of beetles alongside bugs, mayflies, caddisflies and lacewings. They also occasionally eat spiders, harvestmen and lice. That level of insight would have been impossible without modern technology.

This really goes to show how crucial good biodiversity is and for that matter, bioabundance too. If we want bats to thrive then there needs to be bat food out there. Without a healthy population of insects, there will be no bats. There may be some who cannot imagine why that would be a problem, but a world without bats would already have slipped over the edge into ecological collapse, bringing with it not just an absence of bats but of most life on Earth.

Where bats feed is obviously going to be directed by where their food is to be found, which in turn gives us very clear guides as to what we need to protect.

Insects will emerge from shelter and from vegetation as the sun sets. This is a key component for bats as well. Hedgerows can be a crucial factor, not just supplying a larder but also a flightpath along which they can travel. Woodland edges, which are in effect the natural analogue of a hedgerow, are also a great place for a congregation of bats and bugs.

When bats feed is also affected by their prey. Perfect conditions are a warm, damp, still night but even

Small fields with tree cover are the perfect bat habitat.

Cow pats provide food for inverts that in turn attract bats.

Flies at sunset over nettles.

Large yellow underwing.

Cockchafer (May b
on oak leaves.

Natterer's bat in wildflowers.

then, insects will tend to concentrate their activities during the first two hours after sunset (think about when you are being bitten most in an evening in a pub garden!) and the same before dawn. This is partly driven by temperature, so when the air temperature is below 8°C, there is a decrease in the amount of the food available.

To give you an idea of the precarious nature of being a bat, rain will cause many flying insects to seek shelter and bright moonlit nights also restrict moth movement. Bats must eat in these conditions, but how? That follows in the next two sections and relies on their capacity to fly and their ability to shout in a very special way!

Greater horseshoe bats.

Alcathoe bat.

Flight

Flight

It is interesting that when Leonardo da Vinci was drawing designs for a flying machine in the late 15th century it was not to a bird's wing that he looked for inspiration, but a bat's.

Comte de Buffon, the 18th-century polymath, has already shown his rather disparaging attitude towards the appearance of bats, and he was equally dismissive of their skills in flight: 'Their motion in the air is rather a desultory fluttering, than flying, which they execute very awkwardly.' It is a great shame he did not know quite what was going on with all that 'fluttering', as these magnificent animals performed feats of flight that put birds to shame. It might have surprised the great man to discover that the fastest flying animal in the world is not a bird but, as you might have guessed, a bat.

The Brazilian free-tailed bat (below) has been clocked at 160km/hr, beating the fastest known bird, the swift, which manages a meagre 110km/hr.

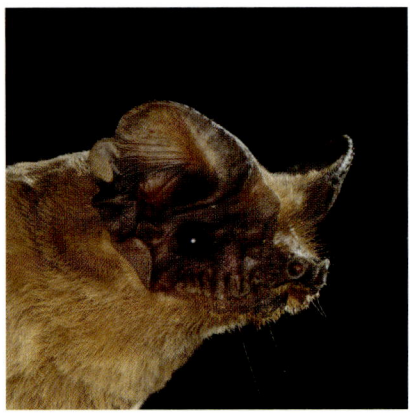

The wing of a barbastelle.

Brown long-eared bat.

Brown long-eared bat.

Now obviously there are some caveats here. This is referencing level flight, but if we are to look at the fastest animal in the sky, that accolade goes to the peregrine, as its stoops have been recorded at 300km/hr. We can't take all the accolades from the amazing swifts either; they still hold the record for the fastest flying bird and also the longest continual flight of any animal, staying aloft for 10 months of the year.

As we established at the start, the name of the order of bats, Chiroptera, indicates it is the hand that creates their wing. They are delicate and sensitive, much like our hands. The wings have many more functions than just flight. They can be used for sleeping bags and raincoats, they hold young, and they can catch food. The smallest flex of a bat finger can alter the shape of the wing, giving them the potential for great agility, far more than the most agile of birds. The thin skin stretched between the 'fingers' is living tissue and can heal when damaged, up to a point. Fortunately, there are wildlife hospitals that can take injured bats and return them to the wild.

Unsurprisingly, different species of bat who live in different habitats have wings evolved to the job in hand. The noctules, who chase down their prey, have long, thin wings that allow them to reach up to 50km/h, however, the more languid brown long-eared bats have shorter and broader wings, allowing them to fly slowly and quietly as they listen for their dinner.

Bats have been described as 'high-performance machines'. Their hearts are up to three times larger than those of equivalent sized mammals. Their blood is rich in haemoglobin to carry oxygen to the muscles and their lungs are more efficient at

Swarming natterer.

extracting oxygen than any other mammal. Flight uses a great deal of energy and bats need to fly to hunt. They are trapped in a cycle of consuming to have the energy to consume, and it is a fine line they walk (well, fly). Key to their hunting is their amazing ability to echolocate, which we will explore in the next chapter.

Grey long-eared bat in meadow.

Echolocation

Echolocation

Bats see with sound. In the same way that humans have to generate light to navigate in the dark, so a bat makes noise.

For us, the light bounces off our surroundings back into our eyes, allowing us to create an image of our environment in our brain. Bats use sound in the same way, allowing them to 'see' an intricate and detailed world by analysing the sound waves that bounce back to their ears and into their brains. If you have ever had an ultrasound, maybe checking on the development of a foetus, the special photograph you clutch and show friends and relatives is the result not of bright lights shining into the womb, but sound.

The level of detail bats can resolve is rather greater than our machines can achieve. They can pluck tiny insects in flight. There is no way they are going to get stuck in your hair, one of the frequently raised concerns when bats are flitting around. It is very fortunate that bats create these sounds at a frequency too high for humans to hear. These tiny mammals use their larynx to power the sound out through their mouth and some can scream at up to 130 decibels, which corresponds to the pain threshold in people.

Bats have evolved an ingenious solution to the real risk of being deafened by their own calls. They are able to flick their hearing on and off while shrieking but quickly enough to be able to pick up the echoes from

Serotine bat.

Brown long-eared bat.

Greenwoods ecohabitat single chamber bat box.

the dark. The system is not perfect, however. When trying to focus on objects very nearby, the call and the echo overlap leading to 'blind spots'. So when hunting this means, as they close in on a moth, the call changes into something with a much shorter sound duration but described by bat experts as a 'raspberry'. When they are just a few centimetres away the bat will rely on either a prediction of where the target will be, or sight; or the use of wings and tail as 'nets' to capture the prey.

As blind as a bat? What nonsense!
Not only can bats actually see really quite well, though not with the same emphasis as humans they are not needing colour or sharpness but they are tuned to their lowlight world, helping them navigate and hunt.

Bats are not the only animal that use sound like this. Whales and dolphins,

Daubenton's bat.

for example, make high-pitched clicks by squeezing air through their nasal passages, which are then focused through their forehead, where a large piece of fat, called the melon, causes them to form a beam. Echoes are picked up by the lower jaw and passed on to the ears, enabling the mammals to work out not only what they are 'seeing' but distance, direction, speed, density and size. Another mammal that has worked out how to echolocate is the wonderful lowland streaked tenrec from Madagascar, which uses tounge clicks at night, while some shrews use ultrasonic whistles.

Daubenton's bat.

How echolocation came about is a subject of great fascination as it sheds light on the evolution of bats in general. For example, it had been suggested that the very different looking and non-echolocating fruit bats might have evolved separately, with some even arguing that as they might have emerged from primate origins. However, this is now discounted. Instead it seems that all bats emerged from the same origin and some bats lost the capacity to echolocate as they specialised in less agile food such as fruit!

Evolution is fascinating. Over millions of years an arms race has been underway with bats evolving more sophisticated ways of 'seeing' potential prey, and those insects in turn evolving techniques to avoid being eaten.

Grey long-eared bat with
privet hawk moth.

For example, various species of hawkmoth stridulate, that is, they generate a noise by rubbing their genitals against their body. This high-frequency sound is used to attract the attention of females, however, it has, over millions of years, been repurposed to also deflect predatory bats. The ultrasound from the moths jams the bats echolocation, causing confusion and a chance for escape. Evolution, of course, is never going to stay still, and there are bats finding ways around this problem. Some are altering the echolocating frequency with which they hunt, taking it beyond the range of the moths' hearing, while others have taken to listening and swooping in to pluck moths from the vegetation.

The brown long-eared bat, for example, is a very good listener. They are also known as the whispering bat. The favourite moth of the brown long-eared is the large yellow underwing. This moth has found a way to escape a hunting bat – when it hears the echolocation it simply folds its wings and falls towards the ground. As a consequence, the bats have started to shout more quietly, hence they are also known as the whispering bat. They also listen very intently with their amazing ears for the sound of a falling moth. The bat then swoops on the moths, scooping them up in their tail basket, a flap of skin that connects the wings at their rear end, and takes them to a quiet spot to feed. They are one of the easier bats to identify from the mess they make, as they will eat the body of the moth and then drop the wings, which, given how many moths they can eat, leads to quite a pile.

Brown long-eared bat.

Lesser horseshoe bat copulating.

Bat Life and Death

Bat Life and Death

All of our bats have to hibernate. The combination of increased energy demands from keeping themselves warm with the disappearance of food as winter approaches mean that this is inevitable.

Before they enter their long winter's sleep, they mate. Females then store the sperm so they do not actually become pregnant until the spring, when the weather becomes warmer.

Hibernation takes place in a hibernacula. For some bats this is a solo affair, but others gather in groups. Hibernation is only the extreme end of their very impressive capacity to tolerate shifts in the weather.

When there is a sudden rush of cold and wet weather during the summer, this will seriously impact the number of bats you will see or hear on food-hunting excursions. We know already what an energetic knife edge they walk (or fly), so what do they do when the insects on which they feed take shelter from the inclement conditions? Bats become torpid in such conditions, but this energy-saving strategy involves them slowing down their metabolism, their bodies cooling. As the temperature rises, so do the bats, and they can get back to work, eating insects. This process is amplified with hibernation.

Lesser horseshoe bats hibernating.

Lesser horseshoe bats with pups.

Hibernating lesser horseshoe bats.

As with hedgehogs, in late summer and autumn bats try to build up fat reserves and some can increase their body weight by up to 35%. Bat hibernation is more complex than that of the hedgehog. They will periodically emerge from the deep 'sleep' of winter to drink, dispose of waste or

Top left: Hibernating bat covered in condensation.
Top right: Greater horseshoe bat hibernating.

move to a better hibernaculum. They live a Goldilocks existence, requiring their spot to be not too cold and not too warm. If too cold they can freeze and die, if too warm, they will be unable to cool their bodies enough to enter the torpid state. This means that hibernacula tend to be humid and protected from extremes of temperature. Caves, mines and the cavity walls in houses can all offer sanctuary.

Pregnant females gather together for several weeks in early summer, forming maternity roosts to have their young, some groups use the same site each time. Pregnancy lasts between six and nine weeks depending on the species and can be influenced by weather, climate and availability of food. Females usually give birth to a single baby each year, which they keep close to them and nurture.

This is a sensitive time for mothers, and if disturbed they can abandon their young. The baby is nursed for four to five weeks until old enough to fly and hunt for bugs themselves.

Below left: Adult females with pups.
Below right: Greater horseshoe bat pups.

A grey juvenile greater horseshoe bat hanging from its mother.

Lesser horseshoe bat
juvenile leaving a roost.

As we know, they fly at night and as dawn approaches they seek out somewhere to snooze away the day. They don't make nests but find places to roost, to hang upside down in peace and quiet. Before humans came along and altered things so dramatically, it would have been the hollows of old trees and caves. Now there are far fewer of these for bats to make their homes.

The alternative has been provided by our buildings, with spaces like attics allowing them to hang from the rafters or secret themselves away behind tiles and boarding. The cycle of life continues, with the males remaining absent from child-rearing duties. After the young have flown, the mission is back to food and building up reserves to survive the rigours of winter.

Brown long-eared bat maternity colony with pups.

It is clear from all of this that bats are vulnerable. During winter days they are at risk from predation and disturbance. While active, they are at risk due to the metabolic tension between the need to fly to catch the food to give them the energy to catch food, and on it goes.

Right: Brown long-eared bat in loft rafters.

Barbastelle tree roost.

Lesser horseshoe and greater horseshoe bats.

Brown long-eared bat.

First Aid for Bats

Bat Life and Death

This is not something that should be undertaken lightly. The Bat Conservation Trust is the best place to find information about what to do.

Their guide, easily found online, starts by saying something really true. 'Finding a grounded or lost bat is a unique experience. For many people, it will be the first time they come close to one of these fascinating and unappreciated creatures. And knowing you've helped a bat survive is a feeling like no other!'

The BCT does not run a bat hospital, but there is a National Bat Helpline that will point you to an expert volunteer. If there are none close by, then the next stop will be the vet.

Although bats are protected by law, you are allowed to handle one in trouble in order to assist it.

The advice is to always wear gloves, as there is a small risk of rabies transmission from bat bites and scratches.

The advice from the BCT is clear:
'A bat needs help, and should not be left or released without advice, if:

- It's on the ground or floor
- It's exposed during the day (e.g., on an external wall)
- It's in the living area of a dwelling, or the public area of another building
- It's been in contact with a cat
- It's a pup without its mother
- It's stuck to something (like flypaper, barbed wire or a fishing hook)

Brown long-eared bat.

Pipistrelle.

Bat stuck to fly paper.

- Its roosting place has been disturbed – for example, by removing wood from a woodpile, taking a sign from a wall or building work.

If you find a bat in any of these situations, please put some gloves on and contain it. Please don't release the bat without further advice. A bat that isn't fit for release, or that is released in unsuitable conditions, is unlikely to survive.'

If you come across a bat in an attic, basement or outbuilding it could well simply be roosting, so do not disturb it, unless it is about to be disturbed, in which case get in touch with the BCT to ensure the law is not broken.

Containing a bat sounds challenging, but it should be quite straightforward. Again, it is the BCT who cover the guidelines. The basics are a shoebox or equivalent with holes punched into the lid, a clean tea towel and a plastic bottle cap. And gloves.

The best advice is to contain the bat as you would a spider, by placing the box on top of it and sliding a piece of card underneath. If that's not possible, cover the bat with a soft cloth, such as a tea towel, carefully scoop it up and place it in your bat care box. (It's especially important to wear gloves if you use the second method.) Put a tea towel or soft cloth in the box for the bat to hide under.

Prepare a bat 'water dish'. Take a small, shallow container such as a plastic milk bottle top or furniture caster and add just a few drops of water (not enough for the bat to drown in). Put this in the box so the bat can help itself to a drink. Make sure the water is topped up regularly. Please do not add any food to the box (bats have a specialised diet and do not need fruit).

Keep the bat indoors somewhere quiet and dark while you call the National Bat Helpline. Please keep pets and children away from the box.

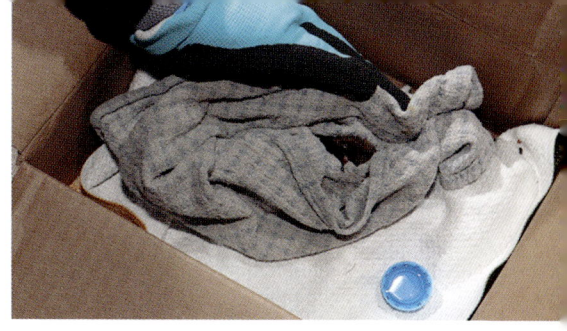

There's no need to give the bat any food, or to put anything in the box besides the cloth and water. Please don't release the bat before getting further advice.

If the bat is not conveniently settled and is still flying around your sitting room, don't try to catch it as it flies – you risk hurting both yourself and the bat. Wait for it to come to rest. If it does that out of reach, you might be able to get some help from the RSPCA or equivalent. The BCT cannot come to the rescue, even if you shine a bright bat sign to the clouds! If you are uncertain, do call them. Remember, they get over 8,000 calls a year... so please don't bother them unless you are really stuck!

Serotine bat.

Threats

Threats

Of course, there are many other threats to bats than being stuck in the house or found wounded in the garden.

First, consider pesticides. *The Silent Spring* (1962) by Rachel Carson referred to the loss of birds, killed by DDT and other pesticides. This spawned the environmental movement and managed to get controls in place that have allowed birds to return. Of course, it was not just birds that were killed. If bats shouted at a pitch we could hear, we might have been very welcoming of the peace that their absence presented.

Those poisons, and others that still exist, accumulate in the fat of bats, concentrating and eventually killing them. They also, as is their 'job', kill insects. Loss of insects has seen a dramatic decline in many insectivo-rous species like hedgehogs, farmland birds and, of course, bats. Antiparasitic drugs given to livestock pass through the guts and are still active in the dung, where they kill the dung-eating insects that play an important part in the diet of many bats.

This, combined with the loss of floral diversity and abundance required by many insects, leaves the amount of food available for bats massively diminished. If we have learnt nothing else from this book, we know that bats live on an energetic knife-edge.

Next to food comes habitat, and in particular the loss of roosting sites. Forestry that does not allow old

Dung beetle aphodiines on sheep dung.

trees to survive and develop holes for roosting is a problem, as is the work to modernise homes by blocking up holes and increasing insulation. This work can also disturb active roosts, which are particularly vulnerable in the summer, as this is when the young are born.

It might seem that roads are not going to present a problem for bats, and for a long time they were underestimated as a threat, but now it is recognised that there are two main problems: collisions and fragmentation.

Collisions might seem easy to avoid. However, research has shown that when bats come to cross a road, they will often keep to the same level above the ground as they were flying as they approached, meaning they can dip into the path of traffic.

Barbastelle road casualty.

For some species though, it is not the presence of busy roads that creates an obstacle but the increased time spent travelling for the bat. Additionally, there is the loss of habitat as new infrastructure is put in place.

The disturbance from roads comes from both noise and light. Light can be a problem everywhere we attempt to reclaim a bit of the night. Some bats avoid artificial light, even at low levels. There is also the complication that street lights can pull invertebrates out of the darker, more sheltered zones in which they would normally be found and take them away from the more sensitive bats.

Wind turbines are a real threat to bats, certainly to individuals. They can be killed by direct collision with blades, and also by the changes in air pressure they generate, but this is not inevitable if an ecologist is involved in the decisions about where turbines are placed.

These things have to be put into perspective – and while some bats will be killed by turbines, this is nothing compared to the numbers killed by cats. Cats don't eat bats, but they do like to play and if they find a roost where they can perch themselves nearby they will swat unremittingly at the poor animals as they fly out to feed. Keeping cats in from dusk to dawn helps protect both wildlife and the cats themselves.

Across the USA and Canada a disease to watch out for is white-nose syndrome, a fungal disease responsible for millions of bat deaths since it was first identified in 2006.

Disease also reared its head in unexpected ways when, with the arrival of COVID-19, came a realisation that there is a little more to our relationship with bats than we might have previously thought.

The Bat Conservation Trust explains how this is not something about which we can blame bats. 'The transmission of a virus (or other vector of disease) from wild animals to humans is normally the result of human alterations to the environment. For example with bats, destroying their habitat (by deforestation and intensive building for example) and the intensification of livestock farming, can mean that bats are forced to live more closely with humans, livestock and pets than they would naturally. This closer contact can result in cases of spillover of a virus into human populations either directly or via an intermediate host (e.g livestock).'

Bat stuck on barbed wire.

Natterer's bat

In the UK there is only one zoonotic disease that is associated with our bats, and that is rabies, which in the past has only been found in Daubenton's bats. Over the last few years another strain of rabies has appeared in serotine bats and there are a few cases each year. BCT states: 'Some bats in the UK carry rabies viruses called European Bat Lyssaviruses (EBLV). EBLV are not the classical rabies virus which is usually associated with dogs; classical rabies has never been recorded in a native European bat species. The presence of EBLV in bats in the UK does not affect the UK's rabies-free status as this relates to classical rabies only.' This is why care is taken when handling bats, and bat workers are highly trained and vaccinated.

Natterer's bats hibernating between bricks.

Whiskered bat.

Bat Conservation Trust
by Alex Morss

Bat Conservation Trust
by Alex Morss

This is a story to illustrate how bats and humans can, with knowledge and support, live together harmoniously.

On a warm evening, if you are lucky and have a bat echolocation detector, you can enjoy an enthralling night choir of 600 soprano pipistrelles singing in the aisles of a grand ancient church, 120 Daubenton's adding their voices from the north porch and a small harmony of super-cute brown long-eared bats whispering from the nave. Smaller colonies of Natterer's, common pipistrelles and Nathusius' pipistrelles may chime in too, set amidst the dramatic atmosphere of the 16th-century Grade 1 listed Holy Trinity Collegiate Church in Tattershall, Lincolnshire.

Over the years, hundreds or perhaps thousands of pups have fledged from maternity roosts safely tucked away here. Unusually, in summer they can even be seen flying during the day (and, curiously, when violin music is playing). The human congregation has learned to make the most of their bat buddies, happily providing a haven and in return enjoying educational and entertaining evenings. The church attracts 34,000 people a year.

Without deeper understanding and expert guidance, Britain's beautiful little acrobats have not always been such welcome church performers.

Daubenton's bat.

Lesser horseshoe bat leucistic.

Their droppings and urine can cause damage to protected heritage features and before BCT's Bats in Churches project began, Holy Trinity was spending £600 a year cleaning up after them.

Like hundreds of other churches, they were guided by us into ways to avoid stains and harm to their beautiful decorative carvings, brasses, woodwork, masonry and the magnificent ancient timber ceilings. Together we have found good ways to dramatically reduce any cleaning burden, achieve repairs or zero-carbon alterations, re-route bat access points or create alternative roosts. All British bats and their roosts are legally protected, they cannot be disturbed, blocked or removed during cleaning, repairs or renovation, but with good guidance, these issues can be resolved.

Old church buildings have been popular homes to bats for centuries and they are now more vital than ever to bat conservation. Amazingly, around three quarters of pre-16th century churches in England have roosts. On average three species are present, and at least 12 species use them. As ever more natural sites like mature trees and caves have been lost, countless generations of bats have taken to the dark, hidden corners of these attractive old buildings.

Weathered gaps give bats access to appealing holey holy hideaways, cosy crevices and undisturbed nooks, spacious old roofs are perfect for juvenile flight practice, sleepy voids and eaves for naps and perfect microclimates. New mums enjoy the warmer spots in south corners for late spring and summer maternity nurseries, whilst in winter the cooler penthouse towers and crypts offer first-class hibernation haunts.

Word gets around. Bats are creatures of habit and highly social, often dwelling in large family gatherings and communicating with one another about where the best 'des res' lifestyle can be found. 'Home' is intergenerational, a furry family affair, and so in come the fluttering congregations in their droves, almost as if they've got the memo from ancient scriptures about being given shelter and refuge in their time of need.

Of course, the surrounding peaceful, leafy, nature-rich graveyards and gardens are often unlit refuges, stuffed with delicious insects and fantastic foraging spots. They provide refuge from the ever-changing modern landscape and more light-polluted urban areas, which so often lack important features such as the mature tree lines and hedgerows needed by bats for commuting. Thanks to their nocturnal nature, you might not even know your secret residents have moved in until you plan maintenance works. Once discovered, however, many people feel honoured and protective of their wild friends.

Between 2018 and 2023, our Churches Project helped hundreds of communities across England find ways of living in harmony with their miniature guests, with some exciting and unexpected results. They became living assets, with bat walks and events drawing in many new visitors keen to care for the grounds and the wildlife. Our work led to an illustrated children's book, school sessions, a Challenge Badge for youth groups and an interactive art installation visited by 5,000 people.

We pioneered two major citizen science projects, surveyed 700 churches and worked on 125 ancient buildings, provided vital insights, free expertise, scientific knowledge and saved at least two churches from closure. We ran workshops and masterclasses on cleaning, bat-friendly timber treatments, surveying, working with volunteers and communities; we provided low-cost protection for historic features, free visits by trained volunteers,

Greater mouse-eared bat.

Bechstein's bat swarming.

free published guidance and free advice via our National Bat Helpline. Another happy outcome was the exciting discovery of two roosts of the endangered grey long-eared bat. Other roosts of local and national significance were preserved, and we mapped church bat distributions across England, creating an invaluable resource for the future.

You can find more case studies on our website and on the Bats in Churches website. These wins for churches, people and wildlife happened thanks to a £5 million partnership between BCT, Natural England, Church of England, the Churches Conservation Trust and Historic England, funded mainly by the National Lottery Heritage Fund.

The other most urgent priorities BCT tackles include: habitat loss, roads, pesticides and the collapse of insect prey populations, chemical treatments of building materials, wind turbines, artificial lighting, climate change, wildlife crime, cat attacks, fly paper and misinformation. We focus a lot of our professional guidance on policy work, public support, expertise, education, research and outreach work in these priority areas.

The big concerns for BCT are all human-driven and therefore overcoming people/nature conflicts are a central theme of conservation work. The Trust was set up by local bat groups in 1991 to provide a national voice for bat conservation and in response to a century of Britain seeing her bat populations crashing. Alongside over 80 bat groups and supporters we are doing everything we can to reverse their current difficulties and help them to recover. We also work more widely with the global bat community to spread understanding, inspiration and action.

Bats are fascinating, remarkable little animals. They represent more than a quarter of mammal species in Britain, and around a fifth globally. Like much of our cherished wildlife, many of them have suffered severe population declines.

The Bad News

The Red List for British Mammals shows four of the 11 species at imminent risk of national extinction are bats (greater mouse-eared, grey long-eared, serotine and barbastelle). Two are near threatened (Leisler's and Nathusius' pipistrelle). Two more are endangered in Wales (Bechstein's and greater horseshoe). We have too little data on three further sparse species to know how much they are at risk (Alcathoe, Brandt's and whiskered).

Furthermore, because some are too rare or elusive to monitor, we only know the population trends for 11 of our 18 species – thanks largely to all the volunteers who support our National Bat Monitoring Programme.

The Less Bad News

Slowly but steadily, chiropteran fortunes are turning for at least some of our winged wonders. Whilst we know there is still a long journey back from huge historical losses (not least because they are typically slow to recover from impacts, with mums usually only raising one pup a year), we do know from our work that 11 of our bat species are at last stable or slowly increasing. We know poor knowledge and misinformation on bats goes back a long way. This is something all bat lovers can help to challenge. Deeply ingrained cultural historical references do not help in this. These mammals have been unjustifiably maligned for all sorts of curious and fictional reasons, ranging from myth, folklore, superstition and spooky Halloween associations to demonic symbolism in paintings throughout history, mentions of shadowy, fluttery spirits flying out of tombs and graveyards. The immortalisation of the world's

Bechstein's bat in a branch.

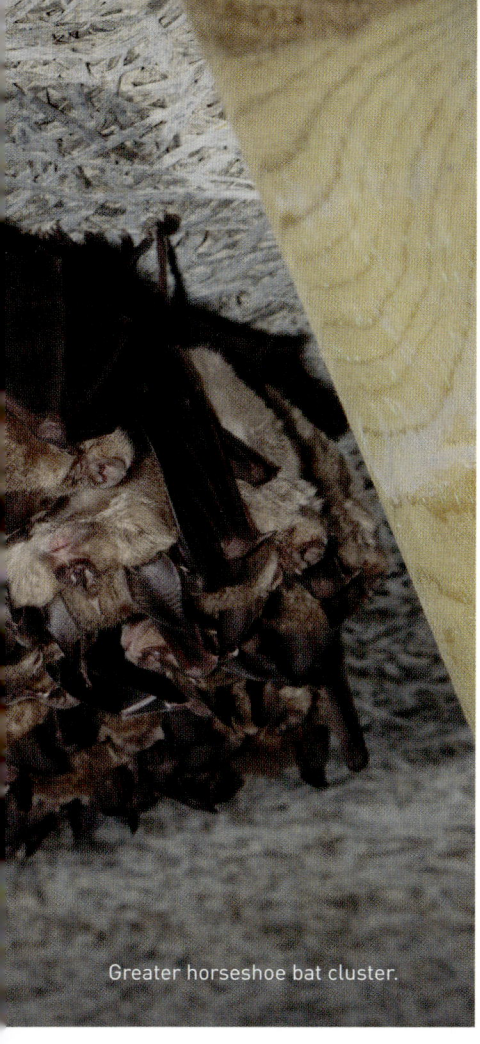
Greater horseshoe bat cluster.

three vampire bat species (out of over 1,400 other bat species) by Bram Stoker's gothic *Dracula* has much to answer for as does the endless 'clickbait-y' nonsense and media scare stories. Even the Pope had a dig at them, condemning bats as creatures of darkness in a famous tweet. He was swiftly corrected by bat lovers around the world!

Those of us who understand do our best to shine a 'light' on the beauty of that darkness and the wonders of elusive nocturnal life which we can all delight in. In return, bats provide invaluable benefits to nature and human communities: pollinating plants and food crops, serving up free insect control on farms, free fertiliser, regulating ecosystems, creating forests by dispersing seeds, bringing us joy, scientific understanding, tourism and visitors who are intrigued by them, and enriching us with biodiversity, natural heritage and cultural inspiration.

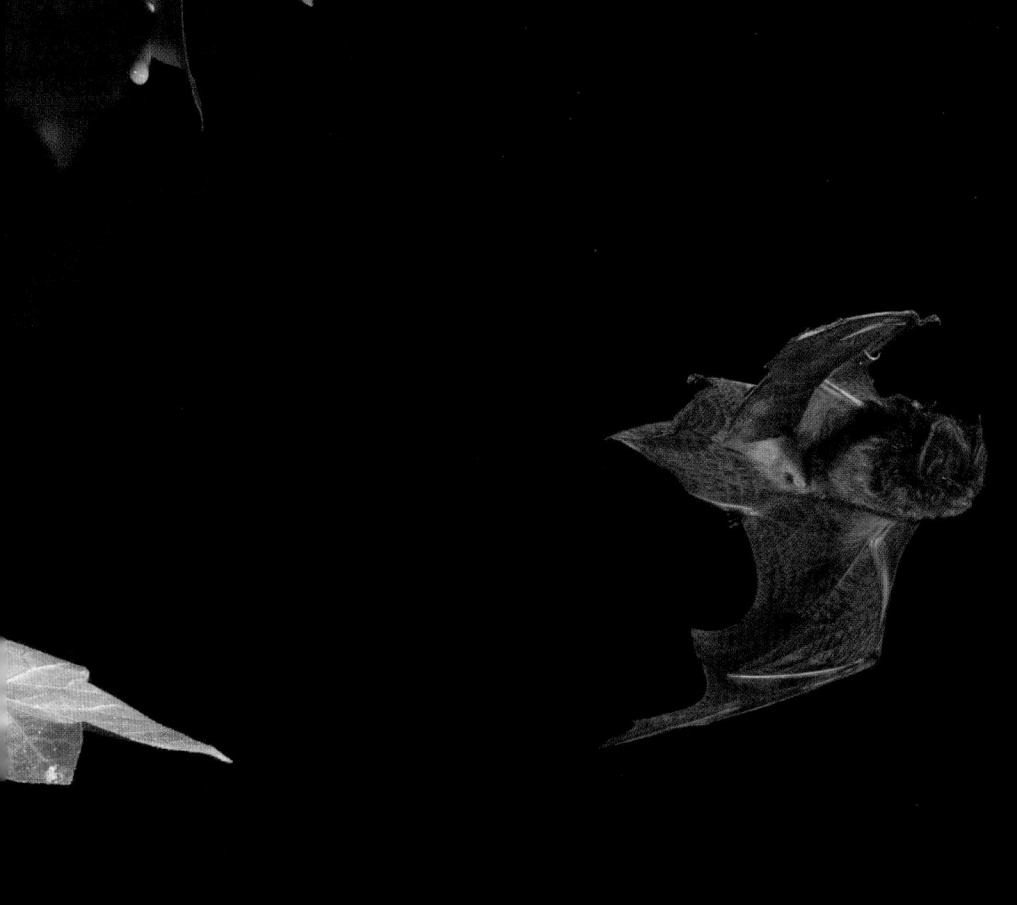

Barbastelle in flight.

Brandt's bat.

Greater mouse-eared bat.

Woman's bat medallion ceremonial robe from the first half of the 18th century, China. This robe carries a symbolic message of good fortune, with the roundels of five interlocking bats surrounding the Chinese character for 'longevity'.

Bats in Myth and Legend

Bats in Myth and Legend

Bats have a bad reputation. Even in these more enlightened times, many people have an unnecessary fear of these amazing animals.

However, it is understandable that something so very different should, in the absence of science, provoke unease.

Across the globe, mostly, bats bring with them disgust, loathing and fear. This deep-rooted revulsion occurred long before stories of blood-sucking vampire bats made it to the Old World.

Some of the earliest representations of bats are from around 2000 BCE, found in Ancient Egyptian tomb paintings. However, despite their extraordinary nature, bats are not given a lot of attention in the Bible. There are three references: first in Deuteronomy, where they are part of the list of things that you must not eat: '...these are the ones that you shall not eat: the eagle, the vulture, the osprey...(lots and lots of other birds) ... the stork, the heron of any kind; the hoopoe and the bat.'

The list is repeated in Leviticus, and the only other appearance comes in Isaiah when it is said, 'On that day people will throw away to the moles and to the bats their idols of silver and their idols of gold, which they made for themselves to worship.' What moles and bats will want with silver and gold idols is anyone's guess!

ctur no cantu mesti paupratis mulcet affectu 7 qamus suam
ratem lucerne no possit unitari: unitatur tn ea sedulitate pi
etatis ·

Bats, from *Northumberland Bestiary*, medieval
illuminated manuscript, 1250–1260.

The Celts

The Celts are responsible for link between bats and what we now call Halloween, celebrated on the 31 October. They called the festival Samhain but it was at the same time of year and they believed that at this time, the veil between this world and the 'other' or afterlife was at its thinnest. A large bonfire would be built on sacred hills and spaces and people would proffer up samples of their crops and the bones of culled animals as offerings to the gods. It can be easily understood that on seeing bats fluttering through the smoke and glimmer of their bonfires, that they might think they could move between worlds and that they might even be the spirits of those departed this life.

In ancient civilizations across the globe, caves were perceived as the doorway to the 'underworld'.

Bats leaving a roost at twilight might mean they are from the underworld too, it is easy to see how they might have been associated with death.

Any dark stories concerning bats were given just cause when it was revealed to the horrified British public that there were bats who fed on blood; although in fact only three species of bat do this. It is clear that vampires existed before the knowledge of vampire bats reached the Old World, there have been stories of the dead lusting after blood since the dawn of civilization. The earliest references come from early Babylonian spirits called Lilu, who would hunt newborn babies and pregnant mothers. That word is thought to be linked to Lilith, variously the first wife of Adam and the primordial she-demon.

The word vampire appears in common use in English in 1734 but had already 'existed' prior to this with stories from northern Serbia of the local practice earlier in the century of exhuming bodies in order to kill the vampires. There are words similar to vampire across the Slavic languages, with connections to 11th-century Old Russian. The link between death and vampires is what really caught the imagination. (See page 143-144 in Art and Literature for details of Bram Stoker's *Dracula*.)

Bat Cures

Egyptologists in Denmark have deciphered a 3,500-year-old manuscript which gives instructions for the creation of medicines for various ailments. Bull fat, bat's blood and lizard faeces are in the mixture and, whilst the ingredients may change across Arabian countries to Greece during this period, the lizards and bats are a constant whenever medicines were made in this area of the world.

Even in modern times the bat is still eaten for medicinal purposes. A study from Texas Tech University published in February 2022, found of the 453 reports submitted, asthma was the most common ailment targeted. This research was aiming to discover a replacement, to prevent the culling of bats for medicinal reasons.

Why Bats Come Out at Night

The Bat and the Rat

A traditional and well-known folktale from southern Nigeria explains why bats fly at night.

The bush rat Oyot and the bat Emiong were good chums who often shared a delicious meal, more often cooked by the bat. One day, when one of Emiong's wonderful soups was on offer, Oyot asked him how his soups gained their unparalleled flavour. The bat told his friend the secret ingredient was himself and that he boiled himself in the water for that added something.

Following a request from Oyot, Emiong took him to the kitchen and, making sure the stock was hot but not boiling, he jumped in, flailing his claws to make it look like it was. When, following Emiong's instructions, Oyot left the kitchen, Emiong jumped from the water and finished making the soup... which was considered delicious by them both.

When he got back home later, Oyot told his wife about the way the soup was created and offered to show her. However, when he jumped into the boiling water, it killed him. His distraught and furious wife ran straight to the village king and he, in his anger at the deception of Emiong, ordered the villagers to find the bat. A posse set off, but Emiong was very elusive and managed to evade them, hiding and only coming out at night. Finally, the villagers took revenge on all bats, and so bats found it better to only come out at night.

The Unhappy Birds

India also has an explanation of why bats only come out at night. Bats

Emiong in pot
by Jane Russ.

Common pipistrelle.

were birds but wanted to become human so prayed to be changed. Finally, their prayers were answered and they were given monstrously ugly human-like faces, with hair and teeth. Flying was still possible as they had wings. The poor bats felt ashamed that they were now neither handsome birds or elegant humans. They only came out at night and spent the daylight hours praying to become birds again.

Madeira pipistrelle.

Bats Help Farmers

In the legendary sense, it has always been held as fact that bats help farmers control the pests on their farms. Now, a study from the Department of Biology, University of Oxford dated 17 April 2024 has confirmed the long-held belief that bats do in fact eat agricultural pests that damage crops. The study was based on the subtropical island of Madeira, an autonomous region of Portugal. The three bats studied that live on the island were the Madeira pipistrelle (*Pipistrellus maderensis*), the Madeira lesser noctule (*Nyctalus leisleri verrucosus*) and the grey long-eared bat (*Plecotus austriacus*).

DNA samples from bat faeces showed that the three subjects had very varied diets, including beetles, butterflies, flies, moths, and spiders. Of the identified species eaten, 40% were likely or confirmed agricultural or forestry pests.

This fact came as a surprise to Angelina Gonçalves (University of Porto, Portugal), who said they had thought that nocturnal butterflies would be the main food source.

This study shows that in an ever enlarging agricultural world, encouraging these amazing little carnivores can be beneficial to society as a whole. The co-author of the study, Associate Professor Ricardo Rocha (Department of Biology, University of Oxford), commented, 'An increasing number of farmers are using bat boxes to attract insectivorous bats to their fields. During our study, we experimented by placing some in the protected area where we were working, and to our excitement, some of these are now inhabited by the vulnerable Madeiran pipistrelles. This suggests that deploying simple artificial bat roosts might lead to win-win outcomes for both conservation and local farmers.'

And finally, a modern legend

The Congress Avenue Bridge in Austin, Texas, is the summer home to North America's largest urban bat colony, an estimated 1.5 million Mexican free-tailed bats. About 100,000 tourists a year visit the bridge at twilight to watch the bats leave the roost. The population of Austin is 750,000, so there are more bats than humans in the summer months!

Japanese bat and moon (1830), vintage woodblock print by Yamada Hogyoku.

Bats in Art and Literature

Bats in Art and Literature

Distrust of bats is not universal. In China the bat is associated with good luck because the word for bat in Mandarin, *biānfú*, sounds like the word for fortune, *cáifù*.

The bat has therefore featured on many ordinary household objects throughout the centuries in China, particularly decoratively, as illustrated below in white jade from the Han dynasty.

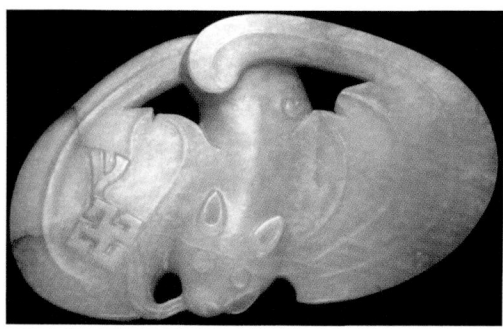

This porcelain bowl (right) showing peaches and bats is typical of the way bats were incorporated into the design of even the simplest of shapes. In the early 18th century the peach colour of this bowl was created by using gold nanoparticles in an overglaze process introduced by Europeans to the imperial workshops. Skilled enamelers taught their skills to the craftsmen so they could create things of beauty for the court. Peaches and bats were often depicted together, the bat being needed originally to deploy the seed of the peach and their use together was a reminder of the cycles of life.

Dish with peaches and bats,
China, early 18th century.

Although, as Japan transitioned to more European clothing, the tradition use of *netsuke* for its original purpose dropped away, the quality of the detailed work and artistry continued to be admired. They were made of many materials: ivory, boxwood, tusk, pottery and, as in this example, just ordinary unspecified wood. However, the subject matter of this particular item is anything but ordinary: in amazingly fine detail if shows a mother with her wing wrapped around her two tiny baby bats. You cannot help but be astounded by the detail and quality of this tiny 19th century piece dimensions 2.5 x 3.2 x 3.5 cm.

Originally, in the 17th century, Japanese wood *netsuke* were the toggles used to hang a small pouch or box to the sash or obi, worn over the *kimono*. These acted as a pocket for the wearer; kimonos did not have pockets. The *netsuke*, hung over the obi and held the *sagemon* (pouch) or *inro* (box) in place. They would be used to hold tobacco, writing equipment or even medicines.

Here is another bat *netsuke* by way
of contrast. This one is in ivory and
slightly larger at 3.2 x 3.5 x 2.2 cm.

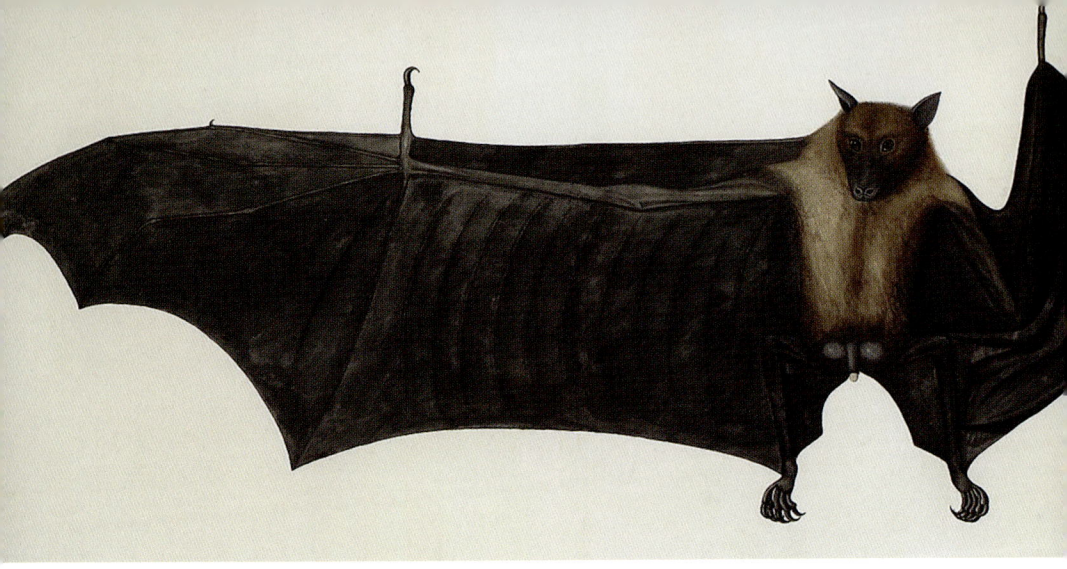

It is inevitable that the nocturnal and mysterious animal was always going to attract attention that might be considered dark. Aesop's Fables contains at least two tales including bats, both of which highlight the different qualities of bats. In *The Birds, The Beasts and the Bat* Aesop builds on the negativity felt towards these amazing animals. As a war raged between birds and beasts, the bat kept switching sides, aligning himself with whoever was winning.

When peace arrived, this duplicitous nature was revealed and the bat was condemned to live a nocturnal life.

'The Bat and the Weasel' underlines this duality of bats. The story tells how a bat caught by a weasel. begs to be released but the weasel says he cannot do this because weasels

Above: Great Indian fruit bat, probably from a follower of Bhawani Das, mid-1700s.

are the enemy of all birds. The bat insists he is a mouse and the weasel, on looking carefully at him, agrees and lets him go. On being caught later by a different weasel, the bat begs for mercy. On hearing that this weasel never lets mice go, he quickly advises that he is in fact a bird, after all, he has wings. The weasel lets the bat go.

Shakespeare

Shakespeare was not going to miss out on the opportunity presented by bats. In Macbeth the three witches' famous incantation, 'Double, double toil and trouble...' includes wool of bat, alongside eye of newt, toe of frog and a fillet of fenny snake in the recipe, one so complex that even Ottolenghi might be stretched (and Waitrose is right out of fenny snake).

Bats pop up in *The Tempest* when Caliban curses Prospero in a most grisly fashion and again, later, in lighter tone in Ariel's famous song:

Where the bee sucks, there suck I.
In a cowslip's bell I lie;
There I couch when owls do cry.
On the bat's back I do fly
After summer merrily.

Above: *Tempest*, Act V, Scene I (Where the bee sucks, there suck I), print by Paul Bommer.

The overall demonisation of the bat, though, is pretty thorough in western stories. Tessa Laird makes the fascinating observation in her brilliant monograph on bat iconography, called *Bat*, that across so many cultures, angels are human in form but depicted with bird wings, while the harbingers of evil come with wings of the bat. An early depiction of this essential characteristic comes in the 1345 painting by an artist known only as Master of the Rebel Angels called *The Fall of the Rebel Angels*.

Of all the rebel angels, it is Satan who has most frequently become associated with bat wings. The reason for the association has to come from the combination of the darkness of the night and the seemingly magical capacity to navigate without sight. But they are not always satanic, in fact it is often in association with depression or melancholia as it was known. Albrecht Dürer's *Melencolia I* from the early 16th century is an engraving that features a bat flying away with the affliction into the sunrise, possibly representing the dawn providing relief from the traumas of a disturbed night.

Albrecht Dürer's *Melencolia I*, 1514.

The Sleep of Reason by Francisco Goya, c. 1799.

In Goya's *The Sleep of Reason Produces Monsters*, from around 1799 (left), bats are joined by owls circling the snoozing artist. The circling nocturnal seem to be there to torment the unproductive writer, asleep on his papers. Goya returned to bats in his sequence of images *The Disasters of War*, created between 1810-20. In plate number 72, *Las Resultas* (the Consequences), he has a bat with an almost human face sucking at the chest of a corpse.

Soon after this William Blake was also taking a shot at the bat for its ability to interfere with a calm existence. In *Auguries of Innocence* he writes:

The bat that flits at close of eve
Has left the brain that won't believe.

Cryptic – yes, but Tessa Laird claims, 'that the bat embodies the damned soul of the infidel, a hangover from medieval Christian imagery...'

The realisation that a bat took this role was too good to miss for the storytellers, though the vampire did not emerge as the dashing seducer until 1819 when John William Polidori published the short book *Vampyre*, based on the story told by Lord Byron as part of the famous competitive story telling contest beside Lake Geneva that also birthed Mary Shelley's *Frankenstein*.

The most famous of the vampires has to be Count Dracula, the creation

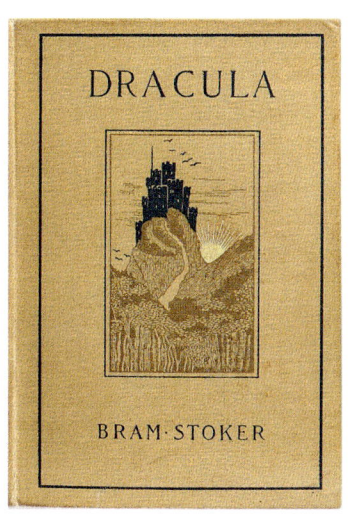

of Bram Stoker following a visit to the town of Whitby.

Gothic literature at the end of the 19th century tended to be full of the eeriness in foreign lands. English Heritage explains how Whitby brought the Gothic to our shores, with its '...windswept headland, the dramatic abbey ruins, a church surrounded by swooping bats and a long association with jet – a semi-precious stone used in mourning jewellery, gave a homegrown taste of such thrilling horrors.'

The bat connection runs clearly through Stoker's vision, 'Then I caught the patient's eye and followed it but could trace nothing as it looked into the moonlight sky, except a big bat, which was flapping its silent and ghostly way to the west. Bats usually wheel about but this one seemed to go straight on, as if it knew where it was bound for or had some intention of its own.'

The mammal provides many good excuses for its demonisation. Stoker was aware of the existence of blood-drinking bats from the New World and as already established, these are an animal that draws intrigue – nocturnal, happy to flit around graveyards, mysterious.

Though there is clearly a little bit of exaggeration at play. 'I have not seen anything pulled down so quick since I was on the Pampas and had a mare that I was fond of go to grass all in a night. One of those big bats that they call vampires had got at her in the night and what with his gorge and the vein left open, there wasn't enough blood in her to let her stand up and I had to put a bullet through her as she lay.' Expecting the exsanguination of a horse by a bat is like a mosquito draining pig, it is just not going to happen but then, why let tedious reality interfere with glorious fantasy!

The word vampire has made its way into many aspects of life.

In *Das Kapital* (1867), Karl Marx offers this description of capitalism: 'Capital is dead labor, which vampire-like, lives only by sucking living labor and lives the more, the more labor it sucks.' The wonderful vampire amoeba, Vampyrella, a genus of single-celled organisms with a distinctive feeding habit. They perforate the cell wall of their target and draw out the contents for consumption.

Films

The legacy of Stoker, Byron, Polidori and many others has reached from literature to the screen. Whether it is Nosferatu in 1922, Bela Lugosi in the 1931 film *Dracula*, the darkly seductive Christopher Lee in the 1958 film of the same name or, more recently, *The Lost Boys* (1987) or *Interview with the Vampire* (1994). In 2008 we first met Eli, a rather ambiguous child-sized vampire in *Låt den rätte komma in* in the original Swedish and subsequently followed in 2010 by an English version, *Let Me In*. Both these films are worth seeing but the Swedish original has the edge, its collection of award wins across the world bears this out. There are so many iterations of the vampire story in film that the Internet Movie Database has a list of the top 150 vampire movies.

Bela Lugosi as Dracula, anonymous photograph, 1931.

Musical bats come in many different forms. *Die Fledermaus* – the German for 'bat' literally translates as flitter mouse, is an operetta by Johann Strauss which premiered in 1874. It is a high spirited romp with a typically improbable tale of a practical joke spinning out of control. There is very little bat action in the opera. The name stems from a Dr Falke, the instigator of the revengeful practical joke, being left drunk in the town square, dressed as a bat and thereafter being known as Dr Fledermaus.

Iconic bats are not restricted to the blood-sucking variety. Arguably even more recognisable is the symbol for Batman, broadcast into the night sky of a dystopian Gotham City, where law and order are challenged and an excessively rich vigilante is looked to for salvation. Batman first appeared in 1939 from the DC Comics empire and was immediately different. He possessed no special powers, other than vast wealth.

As with vampire/Dracula tales, there have been numerous versions of the Batman story in film, television or comic. Adam West was the most well-known Batman (1966-68) until Michael Keaton took over in 1989. While the dark and brooding iterations of recent years tend to stick in the mind, the highly camp 1960s creation is worthy of attention for the laughs.

Adam West, 1967.

The actual bat connections to Batman are limited; other than the bat symbol used to call for rescue, there is the bat cave, the HQ beneath Wayne Manor. The decision to choose this species for his *nom de guerre* came after a bat flapped through an open window while he considered the persona to adopt as he sought revenge on his parent's murderer. The great benefit to (real) bats comes from the portrayal of them as something special, something worthy of respect. Perhaps there are bat conservationists out there who were initially turned on to this nocturnal world by the adventures of Bruce Wayne.

Perhaps the most popular rendering of vampires in the recent past is *Buffy the Vampire Slayer*, a series that ran from 1997 to 2003, which took a twist on the conventional narrative of vulnerable girl hunted by a powerful vampire. Here Buffy Summers, played by Sarah Michelle Gellar, is the powerful girl who

Serotine bat.

hunts vampires. There are often complications in the stories as Buffy is young and in school and as we know, high school passions run deep. This series had a dearth of bats, they appear only occasionally and are not a key plot point, but it remains the best representation of a vampiric world.

Music

There is one bat related tune that can be easily captured as 'nana-nana-nana-nana, nana-nana-nana-nana, Batman!', however, perhaps the most famous comes from one of the best selling music artists of the 20th century, the great Marvin Lee Aday. His legendary voice is perhaps more recognisable under his stage name ... Meatloaf.

The album *Bat Out of Hell* (1977) stayed in the charts for over nine years and has sold over 43 million copies. The phrase 'bat out of hell' is used in reference to the speed and darting movement of someone or something, which come from the evasive nature of bat flight. Meatloaf returned to the Chiroptera in his 1981 song *Blind as a Bat* which lacks most of the drive and interest of his original hit.

Heavy metal singer Ozzy Osbourne famously bit the head off a live bat, while on stage in Iowa in 1982.

Ozzy Osbourne.

It was not quite the malicious act it appeared. The poor man thought that it was a toy bat and made a show of biting it, only to find, 'my mouth was instantly full of this warm, gloopy liquid, with the worst aftertaste you could ever imagine'. He was rushed to hospital and given treatment for rabies 'just in case'.

Of the remaining bat related musical offerings, the best comes from Pat Metheny – one of the greatest jazz guitarists. 'The Bat' was released in 1985 on the album Quartet, featuring other jazz fusion luminaries of Herbie Hancock, Dave Holland and Jack DeJohnette. The piece is gorgeous but it is improbable that a first time listener would associate it with bats!

D.H. Lawrence wrote a long and amusing poem called *Man and Bat* in 1923, though he was clearly not a fan of the animals judging by this extract. The poem was in turn transformed into a song by Howard Skempton, which is beautifully rendered by the baritone Roderick Williams.

Man and Bat by D.H. Lawrence, 1923

A disgusting bat
At mid-morning!...

Out! Go out!

Round and round and round

With a twitchy, nervous, intolerable flight,
And a neurasthenic lunge,
And an impure frenzy;
A bat, big as a swallow.

Lawrence was obviously deeply into bats in 1923 and not in a positive way. This extract is from a different poem but the anti-bat sentiment prevails.

Extract from *Bat* by D.H. Lawrence, 1923

Wings like bits of umbrella.

Bats!

Creatures that hang themselves up like an old rag, to sleep;

And disgustingly upside down.

Hanging upside down like rows of disgusting old rags
And grinning in their sleep.
Bats!

In China the bat is symbol for happiness.

Not for me!

The impact that music has on bats is even less well explored than music inspired by bats but in a paper published in the journal, *Ecological Solutions and Evidence*, in 2023, researchers from the University of Bath and the University of the West of England showed that the noise from music festivals has a substantial impact on the wellbeing of bats.

Some species had their activity nearly cut in half when exposed to loud noise. Now remember the energetic knife-edge along which these animals flit... there is no excess in their lives and losing so much of the time they could be feeding might have serious consequences.

Thomas Nagel entered into the bat cave with his essay from 1974, 'What Is It Like to Be a Bat?'. He was arguing that it is impossible to have a truly objective appreciation of someone else's experience. What would it be like to be a bat? Just try to imagine a world 'seen' through reflected sound; a world in rest that is upside down, a world in flight? He takes this further to argue, somewhat pessimistically, that we have little capacity to truly empathize with other species or even other people. He chose the bat as he considers it to be a 'fundamentally alien form of life.' Alien it may be but the bat is also utterly fascinating and in need of our care and attention.

Right: The 67th plate from Ernst Haeckel's *Kunstformen der Natur* (1904), depicting organisms classified as Chiroptera.

The Bat by Emily Dickinson (1830–1886)

The bat is dun with wrinkled wings
Like fallow article,
And not a song pervades his lips,
Or none perceptible.

His small umbrella, quaintly halved,
Describing in the air
An arc alike inscrutable, —
Elate philosopher!

Deputed from what firmament
Of what astute abode,
Empowered with what malevolence
Auspiciously withheld.

To his adroit Creator
Ascribe no less the praise;
Beneficent, believe me,
His eccentricities.

Amphora bat vase by Richard Freiwald.

The Bat by Samuel Waddington (1844–1923)

Sleek, faery creature,
Strange freak of Nature
That through the twilight comes and goes,
Could we the mystery
Of thy life's history
Resolve, and learn what no man knows,
From what weird forces,
What hidden sources,
Thy winged soul sprang into being
Then might we clearly
Divine more nearly
The world that lies beyond our seeing.

Quaint, mimic angel!
Thy new evangel
Disclose, and share it now with me,
While through the gloaming
Thus lightly roaming,
Thou flittest round this old oak tree;
Tell me what Ages,
What Cosmic stages,
Evolved thy Spirit in the Past;
The far stars glisten,—

Speak, for I listen;
Teach me the Wisdom that thou hast.

Nay, spectral flitter,
Where glow-worms glitter,
Thou art more silent than the sphinx;
Through eras ended
Thou hast descended
Down from the sphere of 'missing links',—
Like pterodactyl
Thy race runs back till
The distance foils our dazèd sight,
To prehistoric,
Rude, allegoric,
Brute offspring of the Infinite.

The Past hath vanished,
From memory banished,
What of the Future canst thou tell?
In words aesthetic,
Sage and prophetic,
Our doubting and our fears dispel;
When life is over
Shall Darkness cover
Thy twilight wanderings with the Night,—
Or from Death's portal

Lesser horseshoe bat
emerging from cave.

Wilt thou immortal
Speed forth into the realm of light?

Mute mystic rover!
Could we discover
Thy wisdom though thou answer'st not,
There is no human,
Or man or woman,
But hath the knowledge thou hast got;

We know we know not!
The gods bestow not
On thee a wider, clearer view;
Thou art surrounded,
On all sides bounded,
By thine own ignorance, – adieu!

Brown long-eared
bat cluster.

Brown long-eared bat carrying a pup.

Photo credits

All photos © Daniel Hargreaves except:

Page 123: Getty Museum collection, public domain.

Page 124: Jens Mahnke, pexels.com.

Page 130: Chris Lawrence/Flickr.

Pages 129, 131, 132: Shutterstock.

Pages 134, 136 (top), 140, 141, 142, 143, 145, 146, 148, 151: Wikimedia, public domain.

Pages 120, 135, 136 (bottom), 137, 138: Metropolitan Museum, public domain.

Pages 139: Jane Russ.

Pages 153: Richard Freiwald.

Endpapers: Linocut by Jane Russ.

Every effort has been made to trace copyright holders of material and acknowledge permission for this publication. The publisher apologises for any errors or omissions to rights holders and would be grateful for notification of credits and corrections that should be included in future reprints or editions of this book.

Acknowledgements

Over the years I have had a few people introduce me to the world of bats – including Huma Pearce, Amy Grace-Fensome, Stephanie Holt, and Dominic Woodfield. There are batty people all over the place, find them!

The team at Graffeg and Jane Russ continue to make magic happen with these little books – long may that continue.

And to Daniel – thank you for making the impossible happen. I had really worried how this book would be illustrated. You have really brought my words to life, thank you.

Hugh Warwick

I could not have helped to illustrate this book without the support of my friends and family, especially my wife Heidi and my parents, who have unwaveringly supported my nocturnal adventures. Many of these photos would not have been possible without the early mentorship from Merlin Tuttle, who taught me the art of bat photography and how to portray these animals as the wonders they are.

Daniel Hargreaves

The world's smallest bat is the Kitti's hog-nosed bat or bumblebee bat. This rare bat lives in western Thailand and southeast Myanmar, where it occupies limestone caves along rivers.

The Bat Book
Published in Great Britain in 2026 by Graffeg Limited.

ISBN 9781802587470

Text by Hugh Warwick and Jane Russ copyright © 2026. Photography by Daniel Hargreaves copyright © 2026. Designed and produced by Graffeg Limited copyright © 2026.

Graffeg Limited, 15 Neptune Court, Vanguard Way, Cardiff, CF24 5PJ, Wales, UK. Tel: 01554 824000. croeso@graffeg.com. www.graffeg.com

Hugh Warwick is hereby identified as the author of this work in accordance with section 77 of the Copyright, Designs and Patents Act 1988.

Printed by 1010 Printing, China.

A CIP Catalogue record for this book is available from the British Library.

This book is designed for general readers, printed with materials and processes that are safe and meet all applicable European safety requirements. The book does not contain elements that could pose health or safety risks under normal and intended use.

We hereby declare that this product complies with all applicable requirements of the General Product Safety Regulation (GPSR) and any other relevant EU legislation.

Appointed EU Representative:
Easy Access System Europe Oü, 16879218
Mustamäe tee 50, 10621, Tallinn, Estonia
gpsr.requests@easproject.com

The publisher gratefully acknowledges the financial support of this book by the Books Council of Wales.
www.gwales.com.

1 2 3 4 5 6 7 8 9

Link to our
Nature Books

MIX
Paper | Supporting responsible forestry
FSC® C016973
www.fsc.org

Books in the Nature Series

The Hare Book

The Fox Book

The Owl Book

The Red Squirrel Book

The Bee Book

The Robin Book

The Badger Book

The Hedgehog Book

The Native Pony Book

The Puffin Book

The Beaver Book

The Otter Book

The Water Vole Book

The Frog Book

The Crow Family Book

The Butterfly Book